TALES OF HEAVEN AND EARTH

Vijay Singh was born in India
not far from the banks of the Ganges.
He is an Indian writer living in Paris.

Illustrations on pages 24–25 and 32: Nicole Carrière
Illustrations on pages 33–39: Gilbert Houbre

Cover design by Peter Bennett

Published by Creative Education
123 South Broad Street, Mankato, Minnesota 56001
Creative Education is an imprint
of The Creative Company

Library of Congress Cataloging-in-Publication Data

Singh, Vijay.
[La déesse qui devint fleuve. English]
The river goddess / by Singh Vijay;
illustrated by Pierre de Hugo;
translated by Gwen Marsh.
p. cm. — (Tales of heaven and earth)
Summary: A mother tells her young daughter how the goddess
Ganga came to earth and became the Ganges River. Explanatory
sidebars present information about Hindu beliefs.
ISBN 0-88682-825-2

1. Ganga (Hindu deity)—Juvenile literature.
[1. Ganga (Hindu deity) 2. Mythology, Hindu.]
I. Hugo, Pierre de, ill. II. Title. III. Series.
BL1225.G35S5613   1997
294.5'13—dc20   96-30890

6 5 4 3 2 1

THE
RIVER
GODDESS

BY VIJAY SINGH

ILLUSTRATED BY PIERRE DE HUGO

C CREATIVE EDUCATION

The beauty of man is often the child that lives on in him.

Day breaks on the immaculate peaks of the Himalayas . . .

It was a breathtaking sight. The icy Himalayan night was coming to an end. As the night dissolved, dawn broke over the peaks. And what a dawn! As though a celestial bluebird with large wings of silk, outstretched, had cast her shadow on the sky. The sky was blue, clear and pure, smiling above the snowcapped peaks stretching their hand toward the heavens. Then arose the sun in the east, illuminating the

Tibet, or the "roof of the world," is in the Himalayas. The highest peak is Mount Everest, at 29,030 feet (8,882 m).

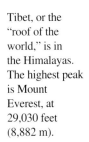

In all traditions, water represents life—it purifies and regenerates. This is why Hindus venerate rivers.

stark beauty of the Himalayas, the tallest mountains ever seen. The most spellbinding view of all was that of a large gaping hole in the glacier, the shape of an enormous laughing mouth, out of which gushed a stream of turquoise waters—singing, splashing, tumbling. This was Gaumukh, source of the river Ganges that Hindus worship as their Goddess.

In the silence and isolation of such surroundings, it was indeed strange to catch sight of a woman and a young girl hobbling toward the river. Clad in traditional Indian tunics and frilled trousers, their heads muffled up in large blankets, they looked like mother and daughter. When they had reached the gaping hole, the source of the holy Ganges, the mother stood before it, bowed and prayed.

The most venerated of all rivers is the Ganges. To bathe in the Ganges at sunrise is the most holy act that a Hindu can perform. Another form of devotion is to float oil lamps on the river. The wish of all Hindus is to have their ashes cast into the sacred waters of the Ganges after their death.

. . . source of the sacred waters of the Ganges.

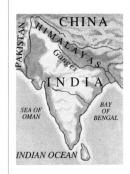

Hindus believe that just as bathing cleans the body, the holy waters of the river wash away the stain of evil, and this is very important if one is to achieve happiness after death.

The mother cast a glance around her to check if a mischievous eye were peeping at them from somewhere. She then removed her clothes one by one, until all she had on was a thin petticoat. She took a quick dip in the freezing waters, chanting "Haregangé, Haregangé." (Hail Ganges, Hail Ganges.) Her voice was, of course, all shivers.

The mother now asked her daughter to take a dip. The perky little girl protested, "Good heavens, no! I'll freeze to death." But her mother finally persuaded her to go in, and the girl took a quick, wet-me-not dip, giggling as she went.

Slipping into a dry set of clothes, the girl now brooded, "Oh, my body feels like ice! Why do you inflict such tortures on me, Ma?" The mother gave her daughter a warm hug and said, "Because a bath in the Ganges will forever make you the purest of human beings. And, you know why." The mother then started recounting to her child the legend of the holy Ganges:

One day, in the celestial kingdom of King Himavat . . .

High in the mountains, below blinding, snowbound peaks and amidst thick, lush jungles, there was once a heavenly kingdom ruled by King Himavat. It was a wonderfully unique land where human beings worshipped animals and birds, and the animals and birds worshipped them; they all lived and played together in utter harmony.

The king had a beautiful daughter called Ganges. She had light almond eyes, arched eyelashes, and lips

like the petals of a budding tulip. Her long black hair was soft and silken and gently wavy. But the most dangerous trait of her body was her bosom. It was said that if the wind blew the veil off her shapely bosom, even the most chaste of Gods was filled with desire for her.

Like all beautiful women, Ganges was aware of her celestial charm, so she was wicked, whimsical, and vain. She even had a cruel streak in her, which is what made people wary of her company.

Ganges had another quality in her: she had a magical touch. Whatever she felt and touched became pure. Her touch could relieve the worst of pains, cure the most incurable diseases and wash away the worst of sins. So people desperately needed Ganges on Earth not for her beauty but for her purifying touch that dissolved all sin.

One day, King Himavat was surprised to find Lord Brahma, the four-headed Hindu God who created our universe, at his doorstep. It was rare for Brahma to pay

Ganges is the sister of Devi, the great goddess wife of the god Shiva. Devi takes various forms and different names, depending on her attributes. The best known are: *Parvati,* (born of the mountains, above), *Uma,* (light), and in her most terrible aspect, *Durga,* (the inaccessible), the slayer of demons.

anyone a surprise visit.

Brahma entered the king's palace and said, "O noble king! No merciful soul would like to see a father an daughter separate, but circumstances are such that people need the presence of your daughter, Ganges, on Earth.

Brahma is one of the three principal Hindu gods with Shiva and Vishnu. But he never became the object of an important cult, and few temples are dedicated to him. The one at Khajurao is the most famous.

Only her divine touch can redeem many a human soul suffering in hell. Can Ganges be sent down to Earth?"

The king could not decline a request from the God who created everything in the world. But out of respect for him, he found it wise to warn Brahma, "It is my duty, my Lord, to send Ganges to rescue the Earth. I must point out, though, that Ganges is whimsical and destructive. She may prove dangerous on Earth."

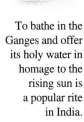

Through this conversation Ganges sat by her father's gilded throne, listening to Brahma, a mischievous smile flickering on the edge of her lips. Ganges loved using her beauty to tickle the gods and their likes.

Brahma repeated his demand and King Himavat agreed to send Ganges. But before Brahma could leave, the king was curious and asked, "What is it exactly that calls for Ganges's descent on Earth, my Lord?"

To bathe in the Ganges and offer its holy water in homage to the rising sun is a popular rite in India.

Hindu divinities are accompanied by familiar creatures called *vahana*. These are symbolic animals such as *Nandi*, Shiva's white bull, *Garuda*, the fabulous bird of Vishnu, Indra's elephant, the peacock of the goddess Sarasvati, and (left) the *hansa*, Brahma's swan.

Shiva, the blue-skinned god, tells King Sagar . . .

On Earth at that time there was an all powerful ruler by the name of King Sagar. His kingdom was vast, and his coffers were full of gold and silver and precious stones. But in spite of his riches, Saga was a sad man; he had no children. For many years the king underwent all kinds of penance and begged the gods to bestow children on his two queens.

One day, when the king was in deep meditation, Lord Shiva, the three-eyed Hindu god who destroys all evil on Earth, appeared before him. Blue-skinned, a cobra

Sagar means the sea, and *Mahasagar* means the big sea, or ocean.

To save humanity from being menaced by demons, Shiva swallowed the deadly poison the demons intended for humankind. That is what made his skin blue.

wrapped around his neck (like a woolen scarf!), a trident in one hand, and standing in a flower of flames, Shiva said to the king, "Do not give way to despair, O suffering king! Your queens will bear you children. The older one will give birth to sixty thousand. They will all be brave and heroic, but they will perish without an heir. Keshini, your younger wife, will bear you just one child, whose descendants will continue your lineage." Shiva then silently sank into the flames.

As the years went by, Shiva's words proved true. The first queen gave birth to legions of sons, sixty thousand in number. Each one grew up to be brave and heroic, proud of their royal descent. And Keshini, the younger of the king's two queens, gave birth to a lone son who grew up to be cunning and unkind. The king did not appreciate his deeds at all.

Sagar was so overjoyed with his sixty thousand brave sons that he became an extremely generous ruler. Every week he opened his coffers of gold and silver and precious stones and gave handsome gifts to the poor. A colossal kitchen

The god Shiva is widely venerated. He is represented in temples by a *lingam*, a cylindrical stone which is round at the top end, suggesting the phallus—the symbol of creation and regeneration. The third eye in the middle of his forehead stands for his perfect knowledge of the truth, and his four arms (sometimes ten) show the extent of his powers.

functioned night and day at his palace, serving rich foods and drinks to the poor and the weak.

Happy at last, the king now decided to organize an *ashwamedha*, a horse sacrifice, as a gesture of gratitude to the gods. This was the most sacred ritual that any king could perform for the divinities. Special arrangements were made. A beautiful white horse, with skin fairer and smoother than the Himalayan snows, was brought from faraway for the sacrifice. The kingdom's most learned priests and saints were invited to read and chant from the holy Hindu scriptures. When the ceremonial fire was lit and the chanting was reaching a crescendo, Indra, the god of strength, always ready to smite dragons and demons, stole into the hall of ceremonies, untied the sacrificial horse standing by the fire, and fled.

"We are doomed!" cried the chief priest, in panic. Indeed, there was no

Sacrifice played an important part in ancient Hinduism, and the horse had a primordial role in old civilizations. To offer the gods a horse as sacrifice was the greatest gift you could make to them.

The god Indra kidnaps the horse that the king was preparing to sacrifice.

worse insult to the gods than an unsuccessful horse sacrifice! The furious king turned to his brave sons, "Go, my valiant sons, and find the horse!"

The sixty thousand princes set out in search of the horse, with just two clues—that the horse was white and that he responded to the sound of "gili-gili-gili-gili." The earth was turned upside down—villages rampaged, woods razed to the ground, mountains and rivers searched. Now and then villagers would wake up to the sounds of the king's children calling to the horse, "Gili-gili-gili-gili." Alas, all in vain. No trace of the white horse was found.

Indra is the god of the atmosphere. He held a central place in ancient Hinduism—he was considered the king of the gods. Today no particular cult is associated with him.

The sixty thousand sons . . .

Ascetics or *sadhus* are men who have given up worldly pleasures in their search for truth. They practice meditation and lead a wandering life, living on alms. An authentic *sadhu* is the object of great respect. Hindu texts claim that *sadhus* have supernatural powers such as foretelling the future, or casting a curse on an evil person.

In low spirits, the king's children were one day sipping water by a sweet-water well, when the eldest said, "I'm sure the horse is deep in the nether world." There was great excitement, for none of them had until then considered searching beneath the earth. So, the princes dug a deep hole through to the nether world and climbed down with the help of a long rope.

According to an ancient idea of Hinduism, Earth was supported by stable, solid elements represented by elephants.

As the king's children reached the nether world, they saw eight gigantic elephants, each the size of a hill, balancing Earth on their backs. The eldest son suspected that the white horse might be near the elephants. He called out, "Gili-gili-gili-gili." The horse did not answer, but the elephants did. This odd sound had given the elephants such a terrible itch in the ears, that they all began to shuffle their feet and flap their ears frantically. So vigorous was the flapping that there was a wild storm in the nether

world, with lightning and thunder. Trees were scorched and uprooted. Up on Earth, there were devastating earthquakes.

When calm returned, the search for the white horse recommenced. It was just before dawn, and the sky was still dark, when one of the princes saw a beautiful

snow-white horse standing by a tree. Nearby, an old man with a coconut beard sat meditating, draped in a long saffron cloth. The princes charged up to the hermit and shouted in chorus, "You dirty old thief! Return our horse!" The enraged hermit stood up, flames of anger leaping from his mouth, "How dare you call me a thief! Phoo!" With one breath, the sixty thousand sons were burnt to ashes.

A hermit is a religious person who has chosen to live in solitude so that he can devote himself to prayer. The word *hermit* comes from the Greek *eremos,* meaning solitary.

With no news from his sons, King Sagar is filled with anxiety.

Since there was no sign of the princes returning, nor any news of them or of the white horse, the king became more and more anxious. Besides, the horse sacrifice was still incomplete, which meant that the anger of the gods could any day cause havoc on Earth. The king was deeply disturbed. Neither his queens nor the soft words of wise men could calm his mind.

Then, one night, he suddenly remembered what Lord Shiva had told him after his penance to have a child: "Keshini, your younger queen, will bear you a child

whose descendants will protect you and continue your lineage." So the king decided to send Keshini's

The elephant is much in evidence in Hinduism, as it was in Indian society. It represents strength and wisdom and accompanies the god Indra.

grandson, Ansuman, a remarkably righteous young man, in search of his sixty thousand uncles and the white horse.

Ansuman was a great lover of animals. Indeed, he had more friends in the animal world than in the human. He could converse fluently with seventy-seven species of animals and birds. When Ansuman was in a jungle looking for the white horse, a friendly elephant came up to him, uncurled his trunk and whispered

A god much loved by Hindus, Ganesh, son of Shiva and the goddess Parvati has the head of an elephant.

chortlingly, "Stop searching in the forests, you fool! The horse is in the nether world."

Ansuman immediately went down the deep hole that his uncles had dug to reach the nether world. Down there, even before he had set his foot on the

ground, another friendly elephant stuck his trunk out and snorted, "There, there, you twit! Your horse is down this alley, standing by a hut."

Ansuman was overjoyed to find the white horse standing by the hut. "Gili-gili-gili-gili," he called out to test if it was the right one. The horse responded with a neigh, and just then, a hermit walked out of the hut. Respectful as he was of his elders, Ansuman saluted the hermit and asked, "O great saint, have you seen my uncles? They had come in search of this horse."

"Yes, I have," said the hermit, pointing to a heap of ash lying there. "They were so disrespectful that I consumed them all with the fire of my penance. All that remains of them is that ash. They are paying for their misdeeds in hell now."

"In hell!" Ansuman let out a cry of anguish, as though an arrow had pierced his heart. Weeping bitterly for his uncles' fate, he clasped the hermit's feet and begged forgiveness for their insolent behavior. The hermit was

Hell, in Hindu mythology, is in the nether world, that is, under the ground. It's a place of utter desolation.

The white horse is found, but the princes must still be saved from hell.

moved by Ansuman's tears and said, "You may take the white horse. But your ancestors' spirits can only find peace if Ganges can be brought down from heaven and her waters touch these ashes. There is no other solution."

Ansuman walked back to the palace with the horse. The king, who had still not been told about his sixty thousand sons, was ecstatic at Ansuman's feat and had the horse sacrifice completed with due ceremony.

The gods are touched by the hardships endured by ascetics in their search for wisdom. That is why they appear to them and are ready to grant their wishes.

It was when the sacrifice was over that Ansuman informed the king of the fate of the princes. The aging king, already in his eighties, was shattered to hear the news. His grief was ever greater, for he knew that no amount of penance on his part at his old age would be able to win Ganges's descent to Earth. He nevertheless decided to leave for the jungle and undergo the worst of hardships, his intention being to persuade Lord Brahma to allow Ganges to flow down from heaven and touch the ashes of the sixty thousand princes.

The king died after a few months without achieving a blessing from Lord Brahma.

Only Ganges, the goddess with the power to purify, can save them.

Now Ansuman followed in the king's footsteps: he vowed to leave the kingdom to his son, Dilipa, and face the worst dangers to win Lord Brahma's favor. His efforts failed to bear any fruit. Likewise, Dilipa failed. Then came Bhagirath, Dilipa's heir, who even refused to ascend the throne, "I will not look at the royal throne until I've brought Ganges down," said a determined Bhagirath, before leaving for the Himalayas.

The banyan tree is held in high esteem: its height is impressive and its roots above ground make it look like a little forest all on its own. Being long lived, it is admired like a wise old man.

Brahma had five heads, a sign that he could see in all directions. He is generally represented with four heads, for the god Shiva, whom he offended, destroyed one with his third eye.

Clad in a tattered loincloth, Bhagirath found a place under a giant banyan tree in the foothills of the Himalayas, and worshipped Brahma. For years he survived on wild berries and grass and braved venomous snakes and deadly scorpions. Oblivious to rain, storm or snow, all the young boy did was meditate and pray.

This single-minded devotion bore its fruit; Lord Brahma appeared before him. "O steadfast one!" said the four-headed god of creation, "Ask for a blessing. It shall be granted." "Then let Ganges flow from heaven, my Lord. Only her holy waters can give peace to my ancestors' souls which are rotting in hell."

Everyone begs the god Brahma to help.

"That is a lofty ambition, my son," Brahma remarked, laughing at Bhagirath's innocence. Ganges's force is such that not even Earth can take it. Only Shiva can." With these words, Brahma disappeared.

Bhagirath now worshipped the blue-skinned Shiva, who appeared before his eyes and asked, "What is it that you seek, O young saint?" "Lord Brahma is prepared to let Ganges descend from heaven, my Lord. But only you can take her mighty force. Help me, my Lord," pleaded Bhagirath, sounding weak and pathetic after a long penance. Shiva, who could destroy anything that was likely to bring harm to the universe, reflected briefly; he knew that Ganges was unpredictable and her moods dangerous even for gods. Nevertheless, Shiva agreed, "I will do it for you. But be careful while conducting her on Earth, Ganges is wild! She does what she pleases. And at times, even she doesn't know what she's doing!"

Everything is ready for Ganges's giddy descent to Earth.

So the stage was set for Ganges's grand descent to Earth. Lord Brahma requested Himavat, Ganges's father in heaven, to let his daughter leave for Earth, and Himavat readily agreed.

As for Ganges, she was only too pleased to leave her parental home; she hated all chains on her movements. She loved freedom, freedom to go wherever she pleased, freedom to play with the minds of handsome young gods and men of noble deeds.

One fine day, Ganges descended, head down, steering

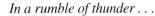

a torrent of surging blue waters behind her. The force of her waters was indeed great and never had anyone seen such a powerful torrent in the skies. Hearing the thunder of the approaching waters, the tigers and leopards took shelter in the caves and the birds shut themselves in their nests. Nothing could be seen in the skies, just Ganges, with all her might, flashing down like a shooting star.

Halfway through her descent, Ganges spotted Shiva in the Himalayas, looking up at her, a cunning smile on his lips. She immediately guessed that the blue-skinned god's intention was to imprison her. "Oh no," shrieked Ganges "He can't rob me of my freedom, I won't let him do it for anything on Earth. No, no, no." And Ganges did one million midair somersaults to lend more

Mountains are always thought of as links between Earth and the sky. So the Himalayas, with the highest peaks in the world, have a semi-mythical dimension for Hindus. Part of the range is Earthbound, part celestial, lost in the clouds, inaccessible— the realm of the gods.

27

. . . she springs free in the Himalayas, but becomes tangled in Shiva's hair.

Ganges's waters escaped from Shiva's hair at various points, forming the different tributaries of the Ganges: the Yamuna, the Baghirathi, the Alaknanda, the Ghaghra, the Gandak, the Ramganga, the Damodara, the Son, the Koshi, and the Chambal.

whirling force to her waters. As the fierce storm of waters came crashing toward the Himalayas, Ganges repeatedly cried out in space, "I'll sweep Shiva down to the nether world. I'll sweep him down to the nether world. . . ."

At last, Ganges struck the Himalayas with lightning force. Men and women screamed on Earth, animals shuddered with fright, but Lord Shiva burst into uproarious laughter—he had trapped Ganges in his black tresses!

Ganges was still too proud to accept defeat. For a whole long year she tried pulling, pinching, biting, scratching, and needling Shiva's head and hair, but the blue-skinned god stayed divinely imperturbable and firm.

Bhagirath begged Lord Shiva

Pacified at last, she flows down to hell and sets the princes free.

to let Ganges free since his ancestors were still suffering in hell, "I will free this cheeky woman for you," said Shiva, "but be careful with her. You have seen how she revels in destruction."

Set free at last, Ganges emerged from Shiva's hair in several streams. Young Bhagirath conducted her most carefully all over Earth, before leading her to the nether world. On Earth, wherever her waters flowed, they brought peace, and whoever took the pain to bathe in them—at Benares, Allahabad, or Hardwar—then their sins were washed away and forgotten. In the nether world, the moment Ganges's holy waters caressed the ashes of Bhagirath's ancestors, their sins were pardoned and their spirits sent to heaven. . . .

The Ganges has three mythical courses: celestial (heavenly), terrestrial (Earthbound), and subterranean (underground).

At the end of the story of the Ganges, the little girl is left wondering.

The mother finished recounting Ganges's legend to her daughter. The little girl, who had listened to the story in utter fascination, now asked, "Does this mean that everyone who bathes in the Ganges will go to heaven, Ma?"

"Yes."

"Even thieves and cheats and bad people?"

"Yes, even they. Ganges's merciful embrace extends to everyone, without exception."

The chill doesn't matter now. Nothing exists but the Ganges.

"So now that I've braved this icy bath, even just for a few moments, will I also go to heaven, Ma?"

"Of course you will. But let me first give you some breakfast, you must be famished."

GANGES: SACRED RIVER

This bust of a man was found at Mohenjo-Daro, one of the most flourishing cities built on the banks of the Indus about 4,500 years ago. This civilization invented a script that has still not been decoded.

To begin with, Ganges was a river, as ordinary or as beautiful as any other. Hindu mythology transformed her into a goddess a very long time ago.

Indus civilization
Indian civilization, one of the oldest, began nearly 5,000 years ago on the banks of a river called the Indus. Early inhabitants of the sub-continent seem to have been a very developed people, living in large, well-planned cities; they even had a script to write in. Their civilization existed until about 3,500 years ago.

The Vedic period
Around this time, another group of people called the Aryans arrived in India from the region of the Caspian Sea and Central Asia. These nomads lived off their cattle and were always in search of new pastures. When they chanced upon a wonderful river, Ganges, they settled on her fertile plains and began to farm.

With problems of food and shelter solved, the Aryans lived calmly, and had time to reflect, think, and create. From these peaceful times came the great Rig Veda, the first literary source of Hinduism.

The dense forests of the plains of the Ganges supplied timber for building and for tools. The river dwellers gradually developed a comfortable way of life.

At Mahabalipuram, a huge sculpted rock (left) depicts the descent of the Ganges (in the center) and Bhagirath in the posture of an ascetic (on one leg, top left).

The civilization along the Ganges river gave birth to Hinduism, which in turn deified the river Ganges.

Delhi

UTTAR PRADESH

Ganges

Ghaghara

Gandak

Brahmaputra

Yamuna

GANGES PLAIN

BANGLADESH

Ganges

Benares

Allahabad

INDIA

WEST BENGAL

Mouths of the Ganges

Calcutta

BAY OF BENGAL

HINDUISM

The term *Hinduism* is not of Indian origin. It was the Muslims who, when they arrived in India in the 8th century, gave this name to the Hindu cults, mainly those dedicated to Shiva and Vishnu.

Indian refers to the country of India, and *Hindu* to Hinduism.

The Vedic period runs from about 1500 to 500 B.C. From then on, gradually, Hinduism as we know it took shape.

Vedic gods were classified as celestial, atmospheric, or terrestrial. Thus, Surya (sun god) represented the sky, Indra (rain god) the atmosphere, and Agni (fire god) the earth. Pictured is an offering of fire at sunset beside the Ganges.

A scene from a *kathakali* dance theater from South India which interprets episodes from the great Hindu epics.

Hinduism evolved over time from a number of cults and popular beliefs, some of which are referred to in the ancient Hindu texts, the Vedas. The Hindu way of life seeks to experience a oneness with God. It began with the earliest Indus Valley cultures.

The Vedic religion

The people who lived in the Indus Valley before the Aryans arrived worshipped fertility symbols: the bull, the mother goddess, the horned god, and sacred trees among other things.

Early Aryans expanded this world of beliefs to include all the natural forces around them that they could neither control nor understand. For example, Agni became the god of fire, the mediator between man and the supreme being. Similarly, rain and sun came to be worshipped.

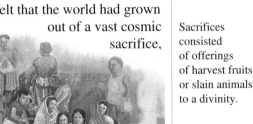

Ancient cults

Sacrifice was the central feature of the Aryan religious life. Small domestic sacrifices were common, but occasionally larger sacrifices were organized in which the entire tribe took part. Sacrifices were meant to win divine favor. The Aryans felt that the world had grown out of a vast cosmic sacrifice,

Surya, the Sun, is the object of a very ancient cult. (Above, the chariot of the Sun, from a miniature of the 18th century.)

Sacrifices consisted of offerings of harvest fruits or slain animals to a divinity.

Priests, or Brahmins, were believed to have magic powers, and they officiated at sacrifices. Because of the importance of sacrifice in Aryan society the Brahmins enjoyed great prestige.

Karma is the belief that all actions have consequences; good thoughts and deeds will lead to a good life whereas bad actions will cause suffering.

and that it was preserved by the proper performing of sacrifices.

Cycle of rebirth

The Aryan idea of life and death was seen in terms of punishment for sin and reward for virtue. This thinking led to the idea of the rebirth of souls, or reincarnation. This meant that happiness and sorrow in this life were determined by a person's conduct in their previous life. Similarly, someone's present deeds would then determine the state of their life after death. People who do not acquire complete perfection, will continue to be reborn, as animal or human being, depending on their past actions. Human perfection can be achieved through yoga, a set of spiritual and physical exercises.

Hindu scriptures

Hinduism is not based on a single sacred book—it revolves around a number of texts divided into two categories: *shruti* and *smriti*.

The *shruti* scriptures are considered most holy because it is believed they were passed on by wise men who heard God's word directly.

The earliest among these are the four Vedas, of which the Rig Veda of the Aryans was the first. These texts, developed over centuries, contain many of the principles of Hinduism. They were memorized by priests and told by word of mouth until they were written down. The Bahmanas supplement the Vedas and give details of how to perform holy rituals.

Texts that came after the *shruti* scriptures are all *smriti*, mostly epics (stories) and songs, written to help Hindus understand the teachings of the *shruti* scriptures.

Two important epics are the Mahabharata, featuring The Bhagavad Gita, which tells about the god Krishna; and the Ramayana, the tale of Rama who, like Krishna, is a reincarnation of the god Vishnu.

Reference dates
About B.C. 2500: Indus Valley Civilization.
About B.C. 1500: Arrival of Aryans.
B.C. 1500-500: Vedas composed. Vedic religion.
About B.C. 1000: Civilization of the Ganges. Brahmana written.
About B.C. 500: Hinduism born.
1st to 5th centuries: Mahabharata and Ramayana. composed.
5th century B.C. to 5th century: *Puranas* written.
From the 8th century: Cult of Krishna and the *bhakti* (devotion).
760-about 820: Shankara, Hindu philosopher.
1836-1886: Ramakrishna, ascetic mystic.
1861-1941: Rabindranath Tagore, writer.
1872-1950: Aurobindo, philosopher.
1869-1948: Gandhi, chief architect of Indian independence (1947).

HINDU GODS

Ganesh, the elephant-headed god, is the son of Shiva and Parvati. He is the god of wisdom and learning. It is he who removes obstacles on the path to perfection. A legend says that he wrote the Mahabharata with one of his tusks.

The gods Krishna (at right) and Rama, incarnations of Vishnu and heros of the two great Hindu epics, are very much venerated today.

It is said that the Hindu religion has thousands or even millions of gods! In other words, they are countless. Hinduism has so many gods because its followers are able to worship all that surrounds them—rivers, mountains, trees, animals. . . . These divinities are really multiple

forms of one supreme being—the Brahman, the universal soul, which is limitless and eternal—the origin of all life. Different gods are only the different images of this invisible reality. By worshipping these forms, a person attains the ultimate goal—union with the spirit of Brahman.

Brahma, Vishnu, Shiva
There are three main Hindu gods. They are Brahma, Vishnu and Shiva.

Brahma is the creator of the universe and everything in it. Vishnu keeps a watchful eye on the universe. Whenever there is the threat of evil on earth, he descends from his celestial home to restore balance. Lakshmi, the goddess of wealth and prosperity, is his spouse.

The third god, Shiva, eventually destroys the universe when it is ridden with evil. Shiva is also the god of dance. His spouse, Parvati, has several names and her attributes change with her names.

(Top center), the god Vishnu, resting on the thousand-headed snake, *Ananta.* Near him, his wife, Lakshmi, and on the lotus flower growing from her navel, the god Brahma.

Sarasvati, wife of the god Brahma, is the goddess of knowledge, the arts, and the sciences.

RITES

A main part of the Hindu rites is the chanting of mantras, or sacred verses. This is accompanied by refined gestures of daily chores, performed to honor God.

Temples

India is home to thousands of *mandira* (temples), some enormous, some small. *Puja*, or daily prayers, are held each evening.

Worship at home

Religion in India is primarily practiced at home. Many Hindu families have a little temple in a special room or in a part of their house. Every evening, the mother or the father of the family lights an oil lamp and offers light, incense smoke, and prayers to the idols of the various gods and goddesses.

Offerings

Offerings are a part of all rituals, and several kinds of offerings are made—water, fire, light, flowers, fruit, *ghee* (clarified butter), incense, or food. Once food has been offered to the gods, it becomes sacred and is distributed among everyone present at the prayer.

In making an offering to the gods, the individual is in essence offering her or himself to the divinity.

One of the steps in the bathing ritual is the offering of water.

Priests look after the altars in the temples.

Meditation in a posture conducive to concentration is a common practice.

FESTIVALS AND PILGRIMAGES

During the festival of *Ramalila*, this boy represents the god Rama.

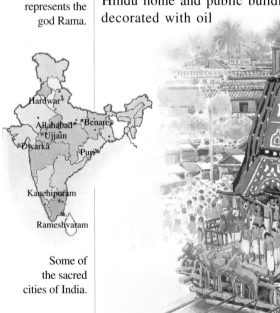

Some of the sacred cities of India.

For *Diwali*, thousands of oil-lamps are floated on the rivers.

Hindus have numerous festivals and pilgrimages all year-round.

Festivals

The *Diwali*, perhaps India's most popular festival, commemorates Lord Rama's return to his kingdom. It is a festival of lights. Almost every Hindu home and public building is decorated with oil lamps. On this night, the country looks like an ocean of pearls!

There are many regional festivals too. Bengal, for instance, holds celebrations to honor the goddess Durga for nearly a month. The region around Bombay worships Ganesh, the elephant god.

At Puri, in Orissa, they celebrate *Rath Yatra*, in honor of Jagannath, who is a form of the god Krishna. Effigies of the god are carried through the streets on enormous wooden wagons, or *ratha*, built like temples.

In the center, *Puram* is celebrated in April-May at Trichur, in Kerala, with superb processions of elephants, fabulously aparisoned, near the sanctuary of Vadakkunathan.

Pushkar Mela, in the Rajasthan desert, brings together thousands of camels under a full moon. Endless streams of camels pull exquisitely carved carts loaded with men, women, children, and harvest to the fair.

The *Trichur Puram,* in the South Indian state of Kerala, is a splendid festival. Prayers and rituals are performed, and hundreds of majestic elephants gather! The antics of the *mahouts* (elephant-keepers) and the elephants are astounding.

Pilgrimages

Kedarnath and Badrinath are two important places of pilgrimage in the Himalayas. The former has a temple dedicated to Shiva, the latter to Vishnu. Both are 11,500 feet (3,500 m) above sea level. It is the dream of any Hindu person to perform this difficult pilgrimage at least once in his or her lifetime.

Far from the Ganges, Tirupati, in South India, has a Vishnu temple visited by millions of people from all over the country. It is also the birthplace of Ramanuja, one of the greatest Indian philosophers.

The world's greatest pilgrimage

Of all Hindu pilgrimages, a visit to the Kumbha Mela is probably the most important. Every twelve years, millions of people assemble at the Ganges to celebrate the victory of gods who, after defeating the demons, recovered the vase (*kumbha*) containing the elixir of immortality.

Each state has its own festivals.

Bengal honors the goddess Durga for nearly a month, ending with the immersion of her statue in the sea. The Bombay region celebrates Ganesh in the same way.

Look for other titles in this series:

I WANT TO TALK TO GOD
A Tale from Islam

CHILDREN OF THE MOON
Yanomami Legends

THE SECRETS OF KAIDARA
An Animist Tale from Africa

THE PRINCE WHO BECAME A BEGGAR
A Buddhist Tale

I'LL TELL YOU A STORY
Tales from Judaism

SARAH, WHO LOVED LAUGHTER
A Tale from the Bible

JESUS SAT DOWN AND SAID . . .
The Parables of Jesus